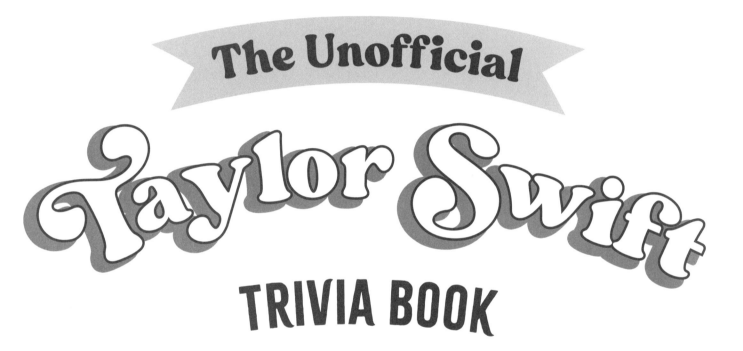

The Unofficial

Taylor Swift

TRIVIA BOOK

www.castlepointbooks.com

The Castle Point Books trademark is owned by Castle Point Publishing, LLC.
Castle Point books are published and distributed by St. Martin's Publishing Group.

ISBN 978-1-250-36186-8 (trade paperback)

Design by Melissa Gerber
Editorial by Monica Sweeney
Front cover illustration by Maurizio Campidelli

Images used under license by Shutterstock.com.

Our books may be purchased in bulk for promotional, educational, or business use. Please contact your
local bookseller or the Macmillan Corporate and Premium Sales Department at 1-800-221-7945,
extension 5442, or by email at MacmillanSpecialMarkets@macmillan.com.

First Edition: 2024

10 9 8 7 6 5 4 3 2 1

The Unofficial Taylor Swift

TRIVIA BOOK

Everything You Need to Know About Taylor with **FUN** Activities to Test Your Knowledge!

CASTLE POINT BOOKS
NEW YORK

getaway car

Welcome to *The Unofficial Taylor Swift Trivia Book*, where you can show off your knowledge and love for Tay Tay. Born on December 13 in West Reading, Pennsylvania, in—obviously—1989, Taylor Alison Swift was destined to become the most influential person of her generation. Taking her cues from The Chicks and Shania Twain, Taylor started off with a country sound that eventually landed her in the Nashville music scene. Her family moved to nearby Hendersonville, Tennessee, when she turned thirteen, to pursue her music career. With more than 200 million records sold worldwide and more than a dozen Grammy awards (and counting) since, there was no turning back.

In the past two decades, Taylor's sound has changed along with her "eras." She has faced relentless scrutiny over her love life, her discipline, her silence, her outspokenness, her beefs, her friendships, her money, her charity, her awkwardness, her poise, her body, her creative property—and her dominance. But after all this, Taylor has proven herself as someone who stands up for what she believes in, who celebrates everyone around her, and who is the best friend in your corner, no matter when you decided you were her fan.

Maybe you tuned into Taylor with her very first hit, "Tim McGraw," off of her self-titled album in 2006; or you tapped your sneakers to "You Belong with Me" two years later; or you felt knowing pangs from "Back to December" and "Dear John" in 2010. Maybe you didn't notice her until her warnings hit too close to home with "I Knew You Were Trouble" off of *Red* in 2012 or you felt a windswept nostalgia from "Wildest Dreams" and get-it-girl empowerment from "Blank Space" in 2014.

Were you one of the latecomers, skipping past her public feuds that propelled 2017's *Reputation* to candy-coated *Lover* in 2019? Or did it not hit you until you were stuck at home in quarantine, letting fairycore storytelling swirl through your ears with *Folklore* and *Evermore* in 2020? But if it's taken you until her inspiring rerecordings—"Taylor's Versions" of everything she's ever written—or even until *Midnights* in 2022, you are safe with Taylor's superfans. Welcome.

On the following pages, you will get to show off your stuff as you listen to *The Tortured Poets Department* on repeat or hang out and make friendship bracelets with friends. Find out which Taylor era is the one that shines for you. Test your T-Swift knowledge with crosswords, word searches, puzzles, and timelines of her boyfriend moments and her badass moments alike. With a mix of fun doodling pages where you can bedazzle your concert attire or read complete biographical rundowns of her successes, you can learn everything you need to know to be a #1 fan.

But this isn't just any book of trivia; it's also a place to record the moments, memories, and inspirations that mean the most to you. Celebrate your favorite albums, songs, and Taylor Swift lyrics. Decide which of her boyfriend red flags are closest to the ones in your own life (just for fun!) and commemorate the meaningful bits of wisdom that she's imparted to you through her crooning voice, humming guitar strings, and vibrant attitude. Being her fan is a lifestyle that can bring tears, comfort, elation, amnesia, and belonging. Connect to your favorite parts of Taylor's incredible, life-long songbook in the trivia and activities to come!

WHICH TAYLOR ERA ARE YOU?

Long live the T-Swift eras. While the moods of her Eras Tour are defined by her first ten studio albums, they are so much more. They are innocence, growth, heartbreak, drama, doubt, regret, love, lust, revenge, freedom, comeuppance, and forever friendship. Look back on her eras below. Grade the eras on scale of one to five hearts, tears, flames, and stars for albums with the biggest surplus of songs that tap straight into your soul.

♥ **Feeling all the butterflies**

💧 **Sad-girl mode and hugs during heartbreak**

🔥 **Power and confidence**

★ **Straight bangers**

TAYLOR!

During the Eras Tour, Taylor was seen with fingernails of ten different colors, each representing one of her first ten albums.

♡♡♡♡♡
◊◊◊◊◊
◊◊◊◊◊
☆☆☆☆☆
TAYLOR SWIFT (2006)
The era of country, curls, innocence, longing, and striving.

♡♡♡♡♡
◊◊◊◊◊
◊◊◊◊◊
☆☆☆☆☆
SPEAK NOW (2010)
The era of putting your mark on the world, of bad boyfriends, sweet boyfriends, forgiveness, and #13.

♡♡♡♡♡
◊◊◊◊◊
◊◊◊◊◊
☆☆☆☆☆
FEARLESS (2008)
The era of heart hands, fairy tales and ball gowns, rhinestones and cowboy boots, starry-eyed success, interruptions, and grace.

♡♡♡♡♡
◊◊◊◊◊
◊◊◊◊◊
☆☆☆☆☆
RED (2012)
The era of red lips and red flags, of BFFs, of standing with your girls and standing in confidence, of maturing, and of beauty.

1989 (2014)

The era of dancing in the limelight, big city moments, bad blood and pettiness, girl power, self-awareness and goofiness, intense romance, and star power.

REPUTATION (2017)

The era of feuds and getting canceled; of licking your wounds and owning your faults; of a dark lip, dazzling snakes, and revenge; of glam, justice, and reclaiming your destiny.

LOVER (2019)

The era of new beginnings, of speaking your truth and Miss Americana, of family love, sunrises, pastel skies, and hopeful hearts.

FOLKLORE (2020)

The era of cottagecore, hibernation, billowing dresses, folk stories and beach towns, of solace and stillness, of introspection and acceptance.

EVERMORE (2020)

The era of champagne problems, of cozy vibes and long braids, of creativity and comeuppance.

MIDNIGHTS (2022)

The era of ghosts, insomnia, and doubt; of explicit tracks and vigilante sh*t, of lavender love and maroon lips, of self-love and adorning yourself in the jewels you earned.

YOUR ERA OF ERAS

Can you guess where you land, bestie?

Add up the total number of ♥ 💧 🔥 ★ from each era. The era with the highest number of colored-in icons is your peak era!

Score

THE TAYLOR WAY TO SHINE

Look how these albums sparkle. There is no stopping Taylor Swift. When her tenth album, *Midnights*, was released in October 2022, Taylor became the first artist in history to occupy all ten of the Top 10 spots on the Billboard Hot 100. When she rereleased her third album as *Speak Now (Taylor's Version)* in July 2023, Taylor earned her twelfth No. 1 album, unseating Barbra Streisand for most No. 1 albums from a female artist. While this list will evolve with future releases, here are some of Taylor's bestselling albums.

Draw your own cover art to show what these albums mean to you!

1989 9X PLATINUM

FEARLESS DIAMOND (10X PLATINUM)

MIDNIGHTS 2X PLATINUM

SPEAK NOW 6X PLATINUM

ENTER YOUR BEDAZZLED ERA

Dance in your living room to her film or sway in the stage lights of a Taylor Swift concert in your most decorated attire. Use this jean jacket as your canvas for the outfit you want to wear. Make yourself feel jeweled up with gems, painted lyrics, or ironed-on images of T-Swift.

PLAN YOUR UPCYCLED CONCERT STYLE

TOOLS, GEMS, PAINT, OR FABRICS REQUIRED:

_____

_____

_____

ALBUMS, LYRICS, PHOTOS, OR SHAPES TO HIGHLIGHT:

_____

_____

_____

The Eras Tour may just be the T-Swift Met Gala. Fans have pulled out all the stops for their concert looks, adding subtle and not-so-subtle details to commemorate their favorite tracks. One TikToker went viral for the jean jacket she decorated with photos of her husband's exes in a nod to the 2023 *Lover* song, "All Of The Girls You Loved Before." (Pro tip: She asked their permission first!)

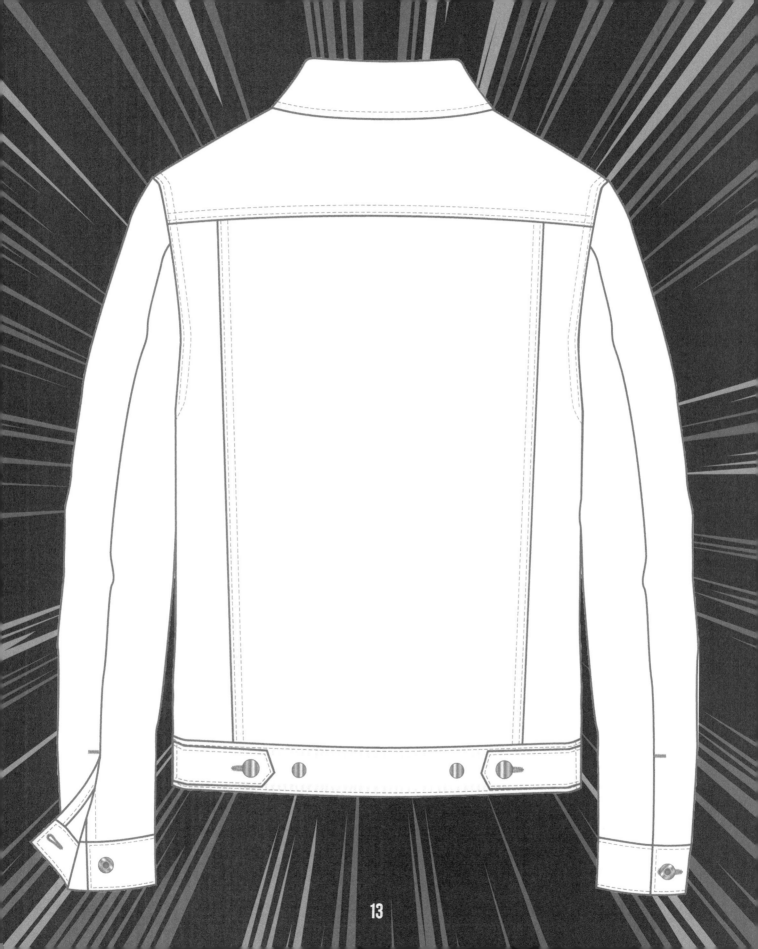

Beginnings Crossword

Always in metamorphosis, Taylor lets her lived experience guide her music style and energy. But her first love was country, and Taylor got her footing as a singer-songwriter by moving closer to Nashville, Tennessee, with her family, where she could have a better shot at a record deal. See if you can answer these questions about Taylor's early days as an artist to complete the crossword!

Across

3 The record label that released six of her albums.

5 The country music inspiration and title of her first single.

6 The number of songs she wrote by herself on her first album.

8 Taylor's favorite lipstick color.

9 The name of Taylor's home state.

10 Taylor's brother's name.

Down

1 On her first time touring, Taylor opened for this country music act.

2 Taylor's lucky number.

4 Her first Grammy win for Album of the Year.

7 The style of music she was first known for.

STRUMMING ON HER GUITAR

SINGER
LIPSTICK PIANO ACOUSTIC
GUITAR
HEART GIRL KOI FISH
RED
STORYTELLER
SOLO
LOVE STORY NASHVILLE
★ MAHOGANY ★
SMILES SEQUINS
BANJO MAHOGANY VOICE
FAIRY TALE DIARY COUNTRY SONGWRITER VULNERABLE TEENAGE COWBOY BOOTS TEARDROPS
NOSTALGIA

You're in Taylor's country chapter, which includes her albums *Taylor Swift* (2006), *Fearless* (2008), *Speak Now* (2010), and *Red* (2012). Let the words of this word cloud stir up memories from your favorite songs or the characteristics she uses in her songwriting that mean the most to you, then write a letter to her based on this era.

Dear Taylor,

_____

_____

_____

_____

_____

_____

_____

_____

_____

_____

_____

_____

_____

WRITE THEIR NAME

Taylor took the power back with *1989*'s "Blank Space." In true Taylor fashion, when tabloids and gossip queens fired up the dating-shaming train about her "long list of ex-lovers," Taylor stopped it in its tracks. This synth-pop departure from her earlier country sounds catapulted her into superstardom, but it's the song's self-aware parody of her romantic life that really hit a nerve, giving women everywhere the power to be proud of their romantic autonomy. Below, describe the kind of person who, when you have a "Blank Space" available, might get their name written in.

_____

_____

_____

_____

_____

_____

_____

_____

_____

_____

_____

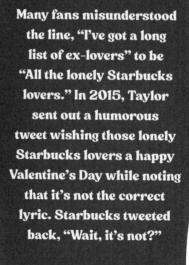

Many fans misunderstood the line, "I've got a long list of ex-lovers" to be "All the lonely Starbucks lovers." In 2015, Taylor sent out a humorous tweet wishing those lonely Starbucks lovers a happy Valentine's Day while noting that it's not the correct lyric. Starbucks tweeted back, "Wait, it's not?"

Taylor's Squad Word Search

Taylor is one of the most popular women on the planet. But it wasn't always that way. Fans know from songs like "The Best Day" off of her 2008 album, *Fearless*, that she struggled with friendships and was often left out of plans and made fun of as a kid. Now she strives to support her squad whenever and wherever she can. Find the names of some of her past and present BFFs opposite.

```
E R S E L E N A G O M E Z Y
F N E M A H N U D A N E L J
F K G N D M B M N L R E Q L
O A D N R I Y P Y X V V M T
N R R M I U D T M I M J B B
O L D Z N V T A L G W J Q P
T I M L T J E E H L Y J K T
N K D M N H K L I I T M B W
A L J R A A Y K E H G R T Y
K O Z I L W D B D D P I V X
C S M B T R Z B D V A O G L
A S Z Y Z J L L L J M R S B
J N G M N T T G G W L B A M
G R B Y Y G N D Z L R M R C
```

Selena Gomez	**Gigi Hadid**	**Sophie Turner**
HAIM	**Karli Kloss**	**Jack Antonoff**
Cara Delevingne	**Blake Lively**	**Lena Dunham**

SONGS FOR SWIFTIES

Solve the song anagrams! The letters of the songs below have been scrambled. Use the clues provided to help you unscramble and discover the song titles.

On her first album, *Taylor Swift*, she wrote this song as a revenge fantasy about a boy who didn't return her affections.

ECTPIRU OT NBRU

Taylor Swift came up with the concept for this song from *Fearless* after overhearing a stranger's argument with his girlfriend.

UOY LGOBEN TIHW EM

In a passing encounter, Adam Young of Owl City charmed Taylor Swift so much that she penned this song for *Speak Now*.

ENTDHCNEA

Jake Gyllenhaal was seen wearing Taylor's scarf, which provided fodder for fans that he is the subject of this song off of *Red*.

LAL OTO ELWL

A recording of Taylor's heartbeat can be heard during this song from *1989*.

DEWITSL ARSMED

Taylor leaned into negative press after a feud with Kanye West and Kim Kardashian. She wrote this song about feeling foolish and rebuilding her image on *Reputation*.

OKOL THAW UOY DMEA EM OD

This song from *Lover* comments on the double standards set up between men and women.

EHT ANM

Fans speculate that this vulnerable song off of *Folklore* is about the sadness and betrayal Taylor felt after Scott Borchetta, label executive of Big Machine and longtime mentor, sold her masters.

YM ARSTE TRIOCCEH

Joe Alwyn's pseudonym, "William Bowery," appeared in the songwriting credits for this song off of *Evermore*.

AAENGHMCP EORLSMPB

Lana del Rey sang the accompanying vocals in this song off of *Midnights*.

WOSN NO HET CABEH

SHE'S NUMBER ONE!

Taylor is no stranger to the top spot. Most artists hit number one when they release a *new* song, but Taylor musters so much fan nostalgia and support that her rerecorded songs sometimes outshine the originals. The melancholic, "All Too Well," was originally released in October 2012 and never came close to single digits. Nine years later, "All Too Well (Taylor's Version)" hit No. 1 upon its November 27, 2021, release. Below you can find ten more Taylor No. 1 hits. Fill in the letters to discover which ones they are!

HAIL THE QUEEN

Taylor is breaking records faster than our hearts can skip a beat. Not only does she have more No. 1 albums than any woman in history, but she even dethroned The King. Elvis Presley previously held the record as the solo artist with the most weeks at No. 1 on the Billboard 200 chart—67 of them, to be exact—from the years 1956–2002. By the end of 2023, Taylor was crowned with this new honor by hitting 68 weeks as a result of the successful rerecording of her fifth studio album, *1989 (Taylor's Version)*.

S_a__ I_ _f_

_l__k __a_e

B_d _l_o_

_oo_ _h__ ___
_ad_ _e _o

C__d_g__

__ll__

A_t_-_e_o

Cr_e_ S__m_r

I_ _t _v_r _o_?
(_a__o'_ _e_s_o_)

__ A_e _e _e __v_r
_e__i_g _a_k _o_
et__r

THE GENRE PENS

With more than 235 songwriting credits to her name (and counting), our beloved Songwriter in Chief is a master of lyrical wisdom, storytelling, flipped perspectives, playfulness, and vulnerability. When she received the Nashville Songwriters Association's Songwriter-Artist of the Decade award in September 2022, Taylor gave a heartfelt speech about her love of her craft and explained her process. She categorized her songs into three imagined lyrical genres: "Quill Lyrics" for the songs that feel like odes to the past, "Fountain Pen Lyrics" for modern songs with evolving perspectives, and "Glitter Gel Pen Lyrics" for playful songs that feel upbeat and delightfully frivolous in every way. Create your own playlists by adding the songs you think best fit these categories.

Quill Songs

Songs about a time gone by with flowery language befitting a Victorian novel or a lost message in a bottle.

_____

_____

_____

_____

Fountain Pen Songs

Modern lyrics with clever wordplay and confessional scenes that bring you into a moment, space, or feeling in vivid detail.

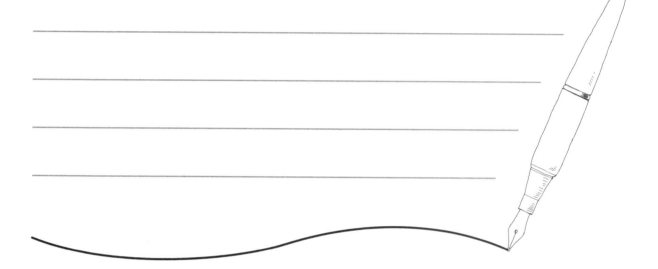

Glitter Gel Pen Songs

These songs are Taylor at her most playful. The lyrics sound like your personal hype girl and act as your permission slip to be carefree, silly, and unapologetically messy.

FOR THE LOVE OF HER GUITAR

From crystals to koi fish, Taylor goes all out for her stylish guitars.
The strumming musician was gifted her very first guitar at the age of 12,
and since then, she's collected more than 100 for her performances and
personal collection. Even Taylor's lyrics pay tribute to the instrument,
with songs like "Teardrops on My Guitar" and "Lover" nodding to
the sadness and scars she's overcome with a guitar in her arms.
Match these iconic string instruments to the songs she's been seen
performing with them by drawing a line to make each connection.

GUITARS

Deering Boston 6-String Banjo

Sparkly Swarovski Crystal
Taylor GS6 Grand Symphony
Acoustic Guitar

Taylor Living Jewels Koi
Acoustic Guitar

Embellished Red Sparkly
Gibson Les Paul Special SL

1959 Silvertone 605 Acoustic Guitar

SONGS

"the 1"

"Last Kiss"

"Mean"

"Fearless"

"Red"

Dazzling Discography Word Search

Taylor's records shine from any angle, but some of her biggest hits almost never came to be or hit roadblocks along the way. The song "I Knew You Were Trouble" from *Red* was inarguably a pop song on an album that was mostly country music. She was discouraged from including it, and critics later claimed that the mix of pop and country made the album sonically messy. It went on to hit No. 1 on the Mainstream Top 40 chart for seven weeks. This success is what drove Taylor to go all in on pop with *1989*. Find her first ten dazzling albums in the puzzle here.

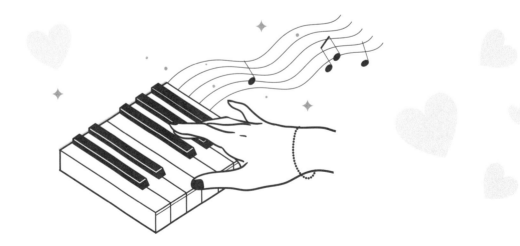

```
T N S S E L R A E F E Y
A W O N K A E P S N W L
Y R X I J Y P D I W T Q
L R N Q T D Y N G S Z E
O E L E D A Y L T Y R W
R K V P E T T H G O X Q
S D M E H T G U L N B G
W Z Z G R I E K P L R T
I Q I Y N M L N O E Q Q
F E R D T O O V I P R J
T Y I E F W E R K N Y V
V M L G D R P B E D N Q
```

Taylor Swift

Fearless

Speak Now

Red

Nineteen Eighty Nine

Reputation

Lover

Folklore

Evermore

Midnights

SWIFTIE BINGO

It's a bingo party! In two teams, listen to a shuffle playlist with Taylor's full discography and cover the bingo board with candy, friendship bracelet beads, or stickers as the songs come on. See who fills out the board first to claim the Taylor crown.

Team One

"ME!"	"PICTURE TO BURN"	"LAVENDER HAZE"	"FIFTEEN"	"FLORIDA!!!"
"TIM MCGRAW"	"CARDIGAN"	"LOML"	"CRUEL SUMMER"	"WILLOW"
"BEJEWELED"	"MIRROR BALL"	♥	"CHAMPAGNE PROBLEMS"	"YOU BELONG WITH ME"
"OUR SONG"	"WE ARE NEVER EVER GETTING BACK TOGETHER"	"BACK TO DECEMBER"	"STYLE"	"ENCHANTED"
"PAPER RINGS"	"MEAN"	"BLANK SPACE"	"WHITE HORSE"	"THIS IS ME TRYING"

AUGUST

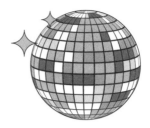

Team Two

"MY TEARS RICOCHET"	"WILDEST DREAMS"	"MAROON"	"INVISIBLE STRING"	"LOVE STORY"
"SHOULD'VE SAID NO"	"SPARKS FLY"	"I FORGOT THAT YOU EXISTED"	"BUT DADDY I LOVE HIM"	"THE 1"
"ANTI-HERO"	"BAD BLOOD"	♥	"YOU NEED TO CALM DOWN"	"ALL TOO WELL"
"THE LAST GREAT AMERICAN DYNASTY"	"FORTNIGHT"	"22"	"NO BODY, NO CRIME"	"LOOK WHAT YOU MADE ME DO"
"THE MAN"	"DEAR JOHN"	"STYLE"	"TEARDROPS ON MY GUITAR"	"KARMA"

COUNTRY MUSIC AWARDS

She may be from a Christmas tree farm in Pennsylvania, but she's a cowgirl in her own right. Here is a list of some awards Taylor received from the Academy of Country Music Awards.

ALBUM OF THE YEAR
FEARLESS
2009

NEW FEMALE VOCALIST OF THE YEAR
2007–2008

CRYSTAL MILESTONE AWARD
2009

ENTERTAINER OF THE YEAR
2011

ENTERTAINER OF THE YEAR
2012

JIM REEVES INTERNATIONAL AWARD
2011

Hollywood Star Crossword

Taylor's autobiographical documentary, *Miss Americana* (2020), and the made-for-theaters production of *Taylor Swift: The Eras Tour* (2023) are serious business, drawing fans everywhere. But Taylor's cameos in feature films and TV shows are the stuff of daydreams. She loves a goofy character or a time to test her acting chops. Find out more about Taylor's onscreen moments in this crossword.

Across

4 She performed a song in the 2009 film based on this Miley Cyrus character.

6 Where she released *Taylor Swift: The Eras Tour* in 2023.

7 Where she released *Miss Americana*.

9 Taylor made a cameo in the season finale of this sitcom.

10 She guest-starred on this crime show.

Down

1 Taylor's film debut was in this romantic comedy.

2 Taylor's character in the film adaptation of *The Giver* by Lois Lowry.

3 She voiced the character Audrey in this animation based on a Dr. Seuss book.

5 She played Bombalurina in the film version of this famous musical.

8 Taylor has appeared as a musical guest and host on this late-night comedy show.

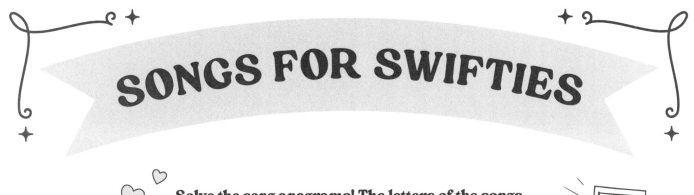

SONGS FOR SWIFTIES

Solve the song anagrams! The letters of the songs below have been scrambled. Use the clues provided to help you unscramble and discover the song titles.

This song was originally written for a talent show her freshman year of high school. It ended up as the final track on her debut album.

RUO GONS

_____

This song from _Fearless_ mentions her best friend from high school, Abigail Anderson.

NEFIETF

_____

Fans suspect that the singer of the track "Paper Doll" is the subject of this song from _Speak Now_.

ERAD OJNH

_____

Gary Lightbody of _Snow Patrol_ contributed to this song on _Red_.

HET STAL EMIT

_____

Katy Perry is widely believed to be the inspiration for this song on *1989*.

DAB LODBO

Reputation is lauded for its in-your-face, uncompromising sound. This song is the only track to feature Taylor playing the piano.

EWN RAYES YDA

Featuring The Chicks, this sentimental song off of *Lover* is about Taylor's feelings of helplessness during her mother's battle with cancer.

ONSO LYOLU TGE TEBRET

Folklore features three fictional characters named after Ryan Reynolds and Blake Lively's children: James, Inez, and the title of this song.

TYTEB

Albums *Folklore* and *Evermore* are connected, and not just because they were released in the same year. This song off of *Evermore* is an extension of the song "Cardigan" on *Folklore*.

OILWWL

The title of this *Midnights* track was inspired by a phrase used in an episode of *Mad Men*.

DRVLNEEA AHEZ

Raising Her Voice Word Search

Speaking from the heart has always been Taylor's forte, but speaking out was not something she was known for in her early career. In the autobiographical documentary she directed, *Miss Americana* (2020), Taylor opens up about how strict management and the fear of angering fans caused her to be tight-lipped about politics and causes she cared about. These days she is a vocal supporter of LGBTQ+ rights and is an anti-bullying champion, women's empowerment advocate, and force to be reckoned with when it comes to unapologetically getting what she deserves. Find the causes Taylor stood up for in the word search.

```
G T N E M R E W O P M E Z
R N K Z L K D N I G L T K
E J I N E Y Z H B T Y T Y
R L X Y K T S D T D H T T
E R J P L R A A L G B T Q
C B K V E L B C I Q C M P
O G Z N B L U R O H B R Y
R P W G A Z Y B A V R M T
D O R G Q P T R I B D V Y
I D E R O R I N D T Y A Z
N L T C W T X M L D N T N
G M V D Y M M J V D V A P
```

Advocate	Charity	LGBTQ+
Rerecording	Anti-Bullying	Copyright
Legal Battle	Empowerment	Ownership

BADASS TAYLOR TRIVIA

In 2015 Taylor wrote an open letter to Apple criticizing a promotional trial that would be free for listeners but leave artists unpaid. Her formidable influence forced Apple's hand, and they changed the policy so that artists would be paid for their work.

Taylor won a sexual assault case in 2017 against a radio DJ who groped her during a concert meet-and-greet. She sued for $1, a symbolic gesture in support of women who have experienced sexual assault but feel pressured to stay silent.

Taylor was critical of Spotify's streaming model and removed her catalogue from the service in 2014. Her outspoken stance that the pay structure was unfair to artists helped change the conversation, leading to more focus on artists' compensation and bolstered support of subscription models. She returned to Spotify in 2017.

Taylor Swift: The Eras Tour film was released in October 2023 during a months-long SAG-AFTRA strike. While other studios had to shut down production entirely, Taylor received SAG-AFTRA's blessing by financing the $15 million dollar film herself and signing an agreement that followed their terms.

A 2019 dispute between Taylor, Big Machine, and new owner Scooter Braun left her without control of her first six albums. Feeling personally betrayed, Taylor began a mission to rerecord all six albums to gain full control of the work and its profits.

AFFIRMATIONS BY TAYLOR

Decorate this page with the gem of wisdom you most associate with Taylor Swift, whether it's a lyric, a line she has said in public, or an example of how she leads her life. Draw this motto out in large, bold letters and use it as your daily reminder to be more Taylor!

HEART WIDE OPEN

You're in Taylor's pop chapter, which includes her albums *1989* (2014), *Reputation* (2017), and *Lover* (2019). Celebrate her evolution into pop through this word cloud of a heart, and fall in love with being at the top of your game. Consider the words on the page and write what emotions these eras stir up for you.

_____

_____

_____

_____

_____

_____

_____

SWIFTIE BINGO

It's a bingo party! The following bingo board is for Taylor's #1 fans. Compare your achievements in two teams and cover the bingo board with candy, friendship bracelet beads, or stickers to mark your earned squares. See who gets "bingo" first to claim the Taylor crown.

Team One

YOU'VE MADE TAYLOR FRIENDSHIP BRACELETS	YOU'VE TRACKED HER EASTER EGGS	YOU ASSIGN T-SWIFT SONGS TO YOUR EXES	YOU GOT TICKETS TO THE ERAS TOUR	YOU SAW *TAYLOR SWIFT: THE ERAS TOUR* MOVIE IN THE THEATER
YOU KNOW WHO OLIVIA BENSON IS	YOU HAVE A TAYLOR SWIFT PLAYLIST	YOU CAN EXPLAIN "TAYLOR'S VERSION"	YOU SAW *MISS AMERICANA*	YOU CRY DURING "ALL TOO WELL"
YOU HAVE "BEJEWELED" ITEMS OF CLOTHING	YOU WERE BORN IN 1989 OR AFTER	♥	YOU CELEBRATE DECEMBER 13	YOU CRACKED THE ONLINE PUZZLES BEFORE *1989 (TAYLOR'S VERSION)*
YOU'VE PAINTED "13" ON YOUR HAND	YOU THINK ENTIRELY IN TAYLOR SWIFT LYRICS	YOU HAD TAYLOR IN YOUR SPOTIFY WRAPPED	YOU CANNOT VISIT ANY CORNELIA STREET OUT OF PRINCIPLE	YOU TELL PEOPLE IT WAS "ENCHANTING" TO MEET THEM
YOU'VE WRITTEN DOWN YOUR FAVORITE LYRICS	YOU FOLLOW TAYLOR'S SOCIALS	YOU USE THE SNAKE EMOJI AFFECTIONATELY	YOU CRY DURING SONGS THAT AREN'T EVEN SAD	YOU SAW *THE TORTURED POETS DEPARTMENT* COMING

Team Two

YOU'VE GOTTEN YOUR HAIR CUT LIKE TAYLOR'S	YOU HAD TAYLOR IN YOUR SPOTIFY WRAPPED	YOU CELEBRATE DECEMBER 13	YOU ARE A PRO AT THE CAT EYE	YOU CAN EXPLAIN "TAYLOR'S VERSION"
YOU THINK ENTIRELY IN TAYLOR SWIFT LYRICS	YOU MISREAD SIGNS AT THE 2024 GRAMMYS	YOU SAW *TAYLOR SWIFT: THE ERAS TOUR* MOVIE IN THE THEATER	YOU FOLLOW TAYLOR'S SOCIALS	YOU OWN HER VINYLS OR CDS
YOU SAW *MISS AMERICANA*	YOU KNOW WHO BENJAMIN BUTTON IS	♥	YOU WERE BORN IN 1989 OR EARLIER	YOU KNOW WHY TAYLOR SENDS KELLY CLARKSON FLOWERS
YOU'VE BEEN TO A TAYLOR SWIFT CONCERT	YOU WEAR RED LIPSTICK	YOU ASSIGN T-SWIFT LYRICS TO YOUR PARTNERS	YOU MUST SKIP ON ANY 16TH STREET OUT OF PRINCIPLE	YOU TELL PEOPLE IT WAS "ENCHANTING" TO MEET THEM
YOU HAVE "BEJEWELED" ITEMS OF CLOTHING	YOU PAINT YOUR NAILS LIKE TAYLOR'S ON THE ERAS TOUR	YOU'VE TRACKED HER EASTER EGGS	YOU'VE MADE TAYLOR FRIENDSHIP BRACELETS	YOU'VE WRITTEN DOWN YOUR FAVORITE LYRICS

(Taylor's Version)

IT'S NOT ALL HEARTS AND ROMANCE

So used to shade that she'll never need sunscreen, Taylor knows how to brush off naysayers who bully her for writing about her past romances. If they paid more attention, these critics might realize many of her songs aren't about love at all. Here's a list of songs that sound like romances but are actually about other issues. Fill in the missing letters as you guess them.

"The Last Great American Dynasty," a quill pen song from *Folklore*, paints a portrait of the former owner of Taylor Swift's seaside estate in Watch Hill, Rhode Island. Rebekah Harkness, a widow and heiress, led a gregarious life that made her the talk of the town. While some details of the song are fibbed (she actually dyed a cat green, not a dog), most are true, from Harkness's ballet foundation to her connection to surrealist Salvador Dalí.

_h_ B_ s_ _ay

S_ve_

R_n_n

In_o_e_t

_ _e M_n

The L_ _t G_e_t
_me_i_a_ D_n_st_

_y T_a_s Ri_o_h_t

M_rj_r_ _ _

M_d W_ma_

_pip_an_

"Marjorie" is a heartfelt ode to Taylor's late grandmother, Marjorie Finlay, on *Evermore*. Taylor weaves a tapestry of her grandmother's love and influence throughout the song, including sage advice repurposed as lyrics on kindness. If you listen closely, you can hear Marjorie's voice in the background music—after all, she was an opera singer.

PIANO MAGIC

Taylor's musical talent doesn't stop at songwriting, vocals, or guitars. She's also an accomplished pianist, and you can spot different kinds of pianos on stage in her performances. Many of these pianos are actually Nord keyboards that have been jazzed up with beautiful shells. Draw a line to match these stylishly embellished pianos to the sets and performances where she's used them.

PIANOS

Mossy grand piano

Wooden upright with floral accents

Black-and-white grand piano with woodgrain pattern

Silver sparkly grand piano

Gold-and-pink grand piano with album title adornments

SETS & PERFORMANCES

American Music Awards

Folklore set

Surprise acoustic set

Reputation set

Formula 1

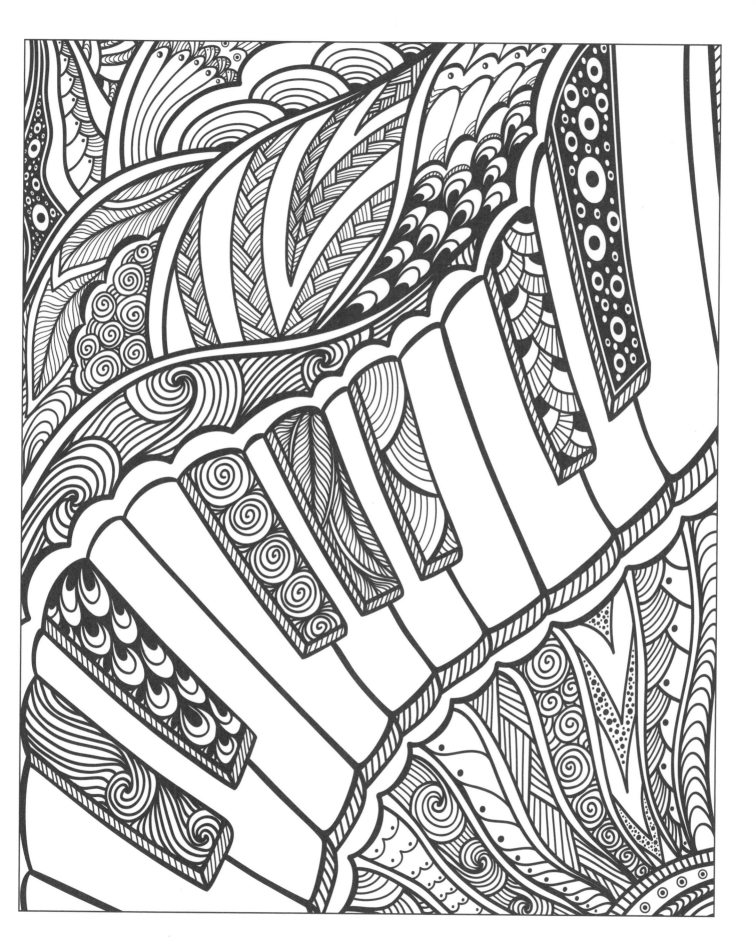

CHECK HER REPUTATION QUIZ

Few artists have feuds with other celebrities so directly connected to the highs and lows of their careers. Take the quiz below to learn more about the famous frenemy who tried and failed to sabotage Taylor over the years.

In 2009, Taylor won the award for Best Female Video at the MTV Video Music Awards for her song, "You Belong with Me." Which artist interrupted her on stage?

Which artist was this celebrity referring to when he said someone else deserved to win the award?

After he received harsh public backlash for his stunt, Taylor extended an olive branch with a song from her album *Speak Now*. Which of her songs represented this show of forgiveness?

In 2016, the song "Famous" off of the album *Life of Pablo* included a derogatory line about Taylor Swift for which the artist in question claimed to have received her blessing. Who came to his defense?

Taylor's public image plummeted after this feud. Two years later, she came back with the album *Reputation*. Which emoji was used against her in the original online spat and later became her symbol of revival?

GRAMMY AWARDS

All that glimmers is gold in Taylor's world. On February 4, 2024, she won her lucky thirteenth Grammy for Best Pop Vocal Album with *Midnights*. She then took home Album of the Year, making her the only artist in history to do so four times. She previously shared the top spot of three wins with Frank Sinatra, Stevie Wonder, and Paul Simon. Take a look at some of her Grammy wins. In the empty stars, write her other "wins" that mean something to you.

ALBUM OF THE YEAR
FEARLESS
2010

BEST COUNTRY SONG
"WHITE HORSE"
2010

BEST COUNTRY SONG
"MEAN"
2012

ALBUM OF THE YEAR

1989

2016

ALBUM OF THE YEAR

FOLKLORE

2021

BEST MUSIC VIDEO

ALL TOO
WELL: THE
SHORT FILM

2023

BEST MUSIC VIDEO

"BAD BLOOD"

2016

Random Acts of Tayness Crossword

Joyful surprises and random acts of kindness are areas where Taylor shines. From surprising fans coping with financial hardship and supporting her fellow artists to visiting hospitals, there seems to be no end to her compassion. See if you can answer these questions about Taylor's charitable giving and kind gestures to complete the crossword.

Across

4 Taylor Swift sent this to a frontline worker during the pandemic.

5 The word for gifts and letters she sends fans.

6 Taylor donated $250,000 to help finance this artist's legal fees.

8 Taylor gave $100,000 bonus checks to each of these members of her Eras Tour crew.

9 What symbolic amount did Taylor request in damages in her sexual assault case?

Down

1 She has donated thousands of these to libraries and schools to encourage literacy.

2 In 2014, Taylor Swift visited this city's children's hospital to surprise young fans.

3 Taylor once attended a fan's wedding in this New Jersey town.

7 She wrote an open letter to this major company in support of artists' compensation.

SWIFTIE BINGO

It's a bingo party! Taylor's catalogue features recurring themes and evokes the full spectrum of emotions. In two teams, listen to a shuffle playlist with Taylor's full discography and cover the bingo board with candy, friendship bracelet beads, or stickers when the clues below occur. See who fills out the board first to claim the Taylor crown.

Team One

PLAYS PIANO	COUNTRY SONG	"GEL PEN" SONG	SONG ABOUT HIGH SCHOOL	PLAYS GUITAR
A SONG THAT MAKES YOU CRY	REFERS TO A BUTTERFLY	TALKS ABOUT BULLYING	THEMES OF FRIENDSHIP	FAIRYTALE OR STORYBOOK REFERENCES
TAYLOR SPEAKS IN THE SONG	SONG THAT ISN'T ABOUT LOVE	♥	"FOUNTAIN PEN" SONG	REFERS TO RED ACCESSORIES, CLOTHING, OR MAKEUP
FEATURES ANOTHER ARTIST	CAUSES AMNESIA	DEFINITELY ABOUT KANYE	DEFINITELY ABOUT AN EX	A BANGER
WHEN SHE WASN'T THE COOL GIRL	DELIGHTFULLY CRINGEY	"QUILL SONG"	THERE ARE SNAKES	CONFIDENT ANTHEM

Team Two

DELIGHTFULLY CRINGEY	TAYLOR SPEAKS IN THE SONG	A SONG THAT MAKES YOU CRY	TALKS ABOUT BULLYING	PLAYS PIANO
THEMES OF FRIENDSHIP	SONG ABOUT HIGH SCHOOL	REFERS TO RED ACCESSORIES, CLOTHING, OR MAKEUP	CAUSES AMNESIA	DEFINITELY ABOUT KANYE
CONFIDENT ANTHEM	COUNTRY SONG	♥	"QUILL SONG"	WHEN SHE WASN'T THE COOL GIRL
FAIRYTALE OR STORYBOOK REFERENCES	DEFINITELY ABOUT AN EX	SONG THAT ISN'T ABOUT LOVE	FEATURES ANOTHER ARTIST	"FOUNTAIN PEN" SONG
"GEL PEN" SONG	A BANGER	PLAYS GUITAR	REFERS TO A BUTTERFLY	THERE ARE SNAKES

Taylor's Loves Word Search

One of Taylor's biggest assets is her ability to be vulnerable, honest, and earnest in her songwriting. She often weaves her past and present romances into the lines of her songs, something critics try and try again to paint as a bad thing. But if you had the privilege of hanging on Taylor Swift's arm and you never showed up in her lyrics, did you even really date her at all? Find the names of some of the people she's dated in the puzzle.

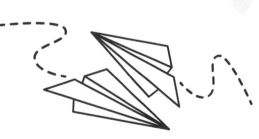

```
J T R A V I S K E L C E J V T
A N A H A R R Y S T Y L E S D
K O L Y J O E J O N A S D T C
E T Z W L X R K J Z Y Y Z A Z
G S P J D O K E R D N K L V N
Y E V V N L R Q Y Y B V J G J
L L B D J M G L W A I D G P P
L D R N G X Y L A N M T N Z D
E D L R Y G A X H U L N Z Y R
N I T D X E D A K L T Y H Y M
H H Y D O Q R V R W M N J O P
A M K J N R Y V X R D W E X J
A O B L I D B J K N P D M R B
L T T S G Y R X R K N D M Q W
```

Joe Jonas   **Jake Gyllenhaal**   **Tom Hiddleston**

Taylor Lautner   **Harry Styles**   **Joe Alwyn**

John Mayer   **Calvin Harris**   **Travis Kelce**

SHINING STAR

You're in Taylor's megastar chapter, which includes her albums *Folklore* (2020), *Evermore* (2020), *Midnights* (2022), and *The Tortured Poets Department* (2024). Her bright light illuminates everything it touches, and you can see why in this word cloud that captures her craft, control, and enduring flame. What about these eras and Taylor's grip on her confidence, her craft, and her worth do you find most motivating or inspiring?

_____

_____

_____

_____

_____

_____

_____

THE BANK OF TAYLOR SWIFT

The "Swift Lift" isn't a feature of a ski resort. It's the term for the financial boom created by the Eras Tour worldwide. With more than 150 shows across the globe, it's the first tour to surpass $1 billion in revenue, and its effects are far-reaching. From driving hotel stays, restaurant reservations, clothing sales, and tourism to the cities where her concerts land to spawning online shops that sell Swift merch and the supplies to doll yourself up, dress the part, and make your friendship bracelets, a multitude of businesses are seeing green. All told, the Eras Tour alone has been credited as contributing more than $4.6 billion to the US economy. Color in the Swift cash below!

A BUTTERFLY IN TRANSFORMATION

Butterflies have fluttered their wings across every Taylor Swift era. From album art and stylish dresses to face paint, jewelry, and lyrics, Taylor has always found a way to show off nature's most delicate winged creature in her work. Then came *Lover*. This album is an ode to butterflies and metamorphosis. Where *Reputation* saw Taylor at her lowest as the "snake," *Lover* is Taylor coming out of her dark cocoon and finding rejuvenation from the beauty of her revival. Here are some of the ways Taylor sent that message to her fans through images of butterflies.

The cover art for "You Need to Calm Down," features Taylor donning a fake back tattoo with a snake in full butterfly metamorphosis.

In the early moments of the "Me!" music video, a snake slithers across a rainbow-brick road only to explode into a kaleidoscope of iridescent butterflies.

Taylor wore butterfly high heels at the 2019 iHeart Radio Music Awards.

In her 2019 performance on the season finale of *The Voice*, Taylor teased the album by performing in front of a massive illuminated butterfly on stage.

Taylor left a "clue" for her fans in Nashville: a beautiful butterfly mural to promote the song, "Me!" In a photo, Taylor stands with arms spread wide in front of the giant pastel painting created by artist Kelsey Montague.

FRIENDSHIP BRACELETS FOREVER

In the song "You're On Your Own, Kid" off of the *Midnights* album, Taylor threads in a line about friendship bracelets. The lyric is a nudge to savor the moment and to have a carpe diem attitude about how you live your life, even when things are hard. This one line launched a friendship bracelet frenzy during her Eras Tour, giving craft suppliers everywhere a boost, and the fashion trend a huge revival. Design your own friendship bracelets with references to your favorite songs, albums, or Taylor references.

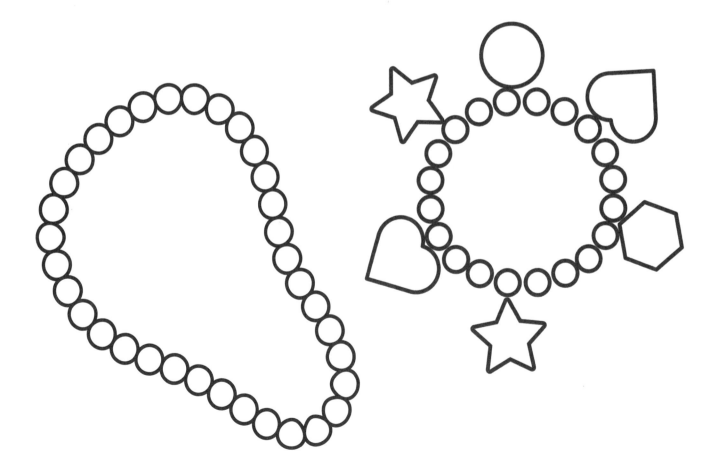

NUMBER 87

Before they began dating, Travis Kelce of the Kansas City Chiefs famously fumbled his meet-cute with Tay Tay. On the podcast he co-hosts with his brother, *New Heights*, he confessed to wanting to give her a friendship bracelet with his phone number on it but was unable to meet her at the show. The rest is history.

SURPRISE, SURPRISE

Made you look. In the lead-up to the 66th Grammy Awards, rumors abounded that Taylor might drop *Reputation (Taylor's Version)*, the rerecording of her sixth studio album. Her white gown with glamorous black opera gloves, an error message on her website with an anagram that decoded to "red herring," and a switch to a black-and-white version of her profile picture made fans wonder if they should be "ready for it." But all's fair in love and Taylor Swift. Instead, as she accepted her lucky No. 13 Grammy Award for Best Pop Vocal Album with *Midnights*, Taylor announced the surprise release of her eleventh album, *The Tortured Poets Department*, on April 19, 2024. In the empty spaces, fill in your favorite fan theories and easter eggs surrounding the album and its songs.

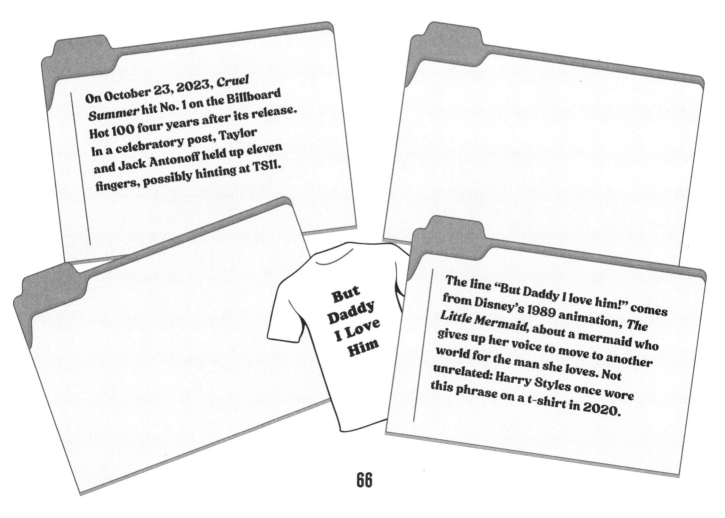

On October 23, 2023, *Cruel Summer* hit No. 1 on the Billboard Hot 100 four years after its release. In a celebratory post, Taylor and Jack Antonoff held up eleven fingers, possibly hinting at TS11.

But Daddy I Love Him

The line "But Daddy I love him!" comes from Disney's 1989 animation, *The Little Mermaid*, about a mermaid who gives up her voice to move to another world for the man she loves. Not unrelated: Harry Styles once wore this phrase on a t-shirt in 2020.

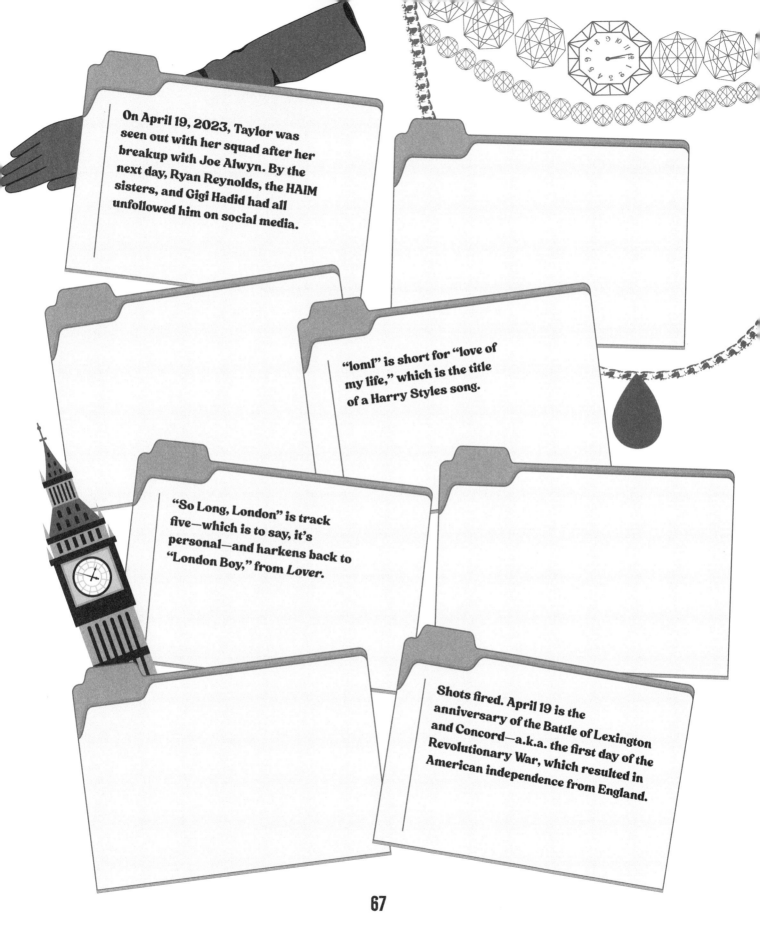

On April 19, 2023, Taylor was seen out with her squad after her breakup with Joe Alwyn. By the next day, Ryan Reynolds, the HAIM sisters, and Gigi Hadid had all unfollowed him on social media.

"loml" is short for "love of my life," which is the title of a Harry Styles song.

"So Long, London" is track five—which is to say, it's personal—and harkens back to "London Boy," from *Lover*.

Shots fired. April 19 is the anniversary of the Battle of Lexington and Concord—a.k.a. the first day of the Revolutionary War, which resulted in American independence from England.

IF I WERE A SONGWRITER

Taylor Swift is more than a singer, she's a lyricist and storyteller. Pore over your favorite songs by this songwriting superstar and pull the lines that have the most meaning to you or that make you bounce in your seat. Reimagine her songs with your own spin, or write out the lines of a song that you think would fit in a Taylor era. Become a songwriter below!

FROM THE DESK OF TAYLOR SWIFT

Number eleven, *The Tortured Poets Department*, is Taylor like we've never seen her before. As you let the sounds of this album wash over you, grade the songs on a scale of one to five hearts, tears, flames, and stars. Jot down the lyrics that jump off of the Chairman's desk and straight into your soul.

♥ **Feeling all the butterflies**

💧 **Sad-girl mode and hugs during heartbreak**

🔥 **Power and confidence**

★ **Straight bangers**

♡♡♡♡♡
◊◊◊◊◊
🔥🔥🔥🔥🔥
☆☆☆☆☆
"FORTNIGHT"

LYRICS YOU LOVE

_____
_____
_____
_____
_____

♡♡♡♡♡
◊◊◊◊◊
🔥🔥🔥🔥🔥
☆☆☆☆☆
"MY BOY ONLY BREAKS HIS FAVORITE TOYS"

LYRICS YOU LOVE

_____
_____
_____
_____
_____

♡♡♡♡♡
◊◊◊◊◊
🔥🔥🔥🔥🔥
☆☆☆☆☆
"THE TORTURED POETS DEPARTMENT"

LYRICS YOU LOVE

_____
_____
_____
_____

♡♡♡♡♡
◊◊◊◊◊
🔥🔥🔥🔥🔥
☆☆☆☆☆
"DOWN BAD"

LYRICS YOU LOVE

_____
_____
_____
_____

♡♡♡♡♡
◊◊◊◊◊
🔥🔥🔥🔥🔥
☆☆☆☆☆

"SO LONG, LONDON"

LYRICS YOU LOVE

_____
_____
_____
_____
_____

♡♡♡♡♡
◊◊◊◊◊
🔥🔥🔥🔥🔥
☆☆☆☆☆

"FLORIDA!!!"

LYRICS YOU LOVE

_____
_____
_____
_____
_____

♡♡♡♡♡
◊◊◊◊◊
🔥🔥🔥🔥🔥
☆☆☆☆☆

"BUT DADDY I LOVE HIM"

LYRICS YOU LOVE

_____
_____
_____
_____
_____

♡♡♡♡♡
◊◊◊◊◊
🔥🔥🔥🔥🔥
☆☆☆☆☆

"GUILTY AS SIN?"

LYRICS YOU LOVE

_____
_____
_____
_____
_____

♡♡♡♡♡
◊◊◊◊◊
🔥🔥🔥🔥🔥
☆☆☆☆☆

"FRESH OUT THE SLAMMER"

LYRICS YOU LOVE

_____
_____
_____
_____
_____

♡♡♡♡♡
◊◊◊◊◊
🔥🔥🔥🔥🔥
☆☆☆☆☆

"WHO'S AFRAID OF LITTLE OLD ME?"

LYRICS YOU LOVE

_____
_____
_____
_____
_____

FROM THE DESK OF TAYLOR SWIFT

♥ Feeling all the butterflies
💧 Sad-girl mode and hugs during heartbreak

🔥 Power and confidence
★ Straight bangers

♡♡♡♡♡
💧💧💧💧💧
🔥🔥🔥🔥🔥
☆☆☆☆☆
"I CAN FIX HIM (NO REALLY I CAN)"

LYRICS YOU LOVE

_____
_____
_____
_____
_____

♡♡♡♡♡
💧💧💧💧💧
🔥🔥🔥🔥🔥
☆☆☆☆☆
"I CAN DO IT WITH A BROKEN HEART"

LYRICS YOU LOVE

_____
_____
_____
_____
_____

♡♡♡♡♡
💧💧💧💧💧
🔥🔥🔥🔥🔥
☆☆☆☆☆
"LOML"

LYRICS YOU LOVE

_____
_____
_____
_____
_____

♡♡♡♡♡
💧💧💧💧💧
🔥🔥🔥🔥🔥
☆☆☆☆☆
"THE SMALLEST MAN WHO EVER LIVED"

LYRICS YOU LOVE

_____
_____
_____
_____
_____

♡♡♡♡♡
◊◊◊◊◊
⟁⟁⟁⟁⟁
☆☆☆☆☆ **"THE ALCHEMY"**

LYRICS YOU LOVE

_____
_____
_____
_____
_____
_____

♡♡♡♡♡
◊◊◊◊◊
⟁⟁⟁⟁⟁
☆☆☆☆☆ **"CLARA BOW"**

LYRICS YOU LOVE

_____
_____
_____
_____
_____
_____

♡♡♡♡♡
◊◊◊◊◊
⟁⟁⟁⟁⟁
☆☆☆☆☆ **"THE MANUSCRIPT"**

LYRICS YOU LOVE

_____
_____
_____
_____
_____
_____

LYRICS TO LIVE BY

You know the ones. Scrawl out the lines that cut deep, that fill you with hope, that invigorate your soul, or that make you feel like it's all going to be okay. Grade the lyrics on scale of one to five hearts, tears, flames, and stars for the lines that made you feel like Taylor really understands you.

♥ **Feeling all the butterflies**

♦ **Sad-girl mode and hugs during heartbreak**

♦ **Power and confidence**

★ **Straight bangers**

♡♡♡♡♡
◊◊◊◊◊
♨♨♨♨♨
☆☆☆☆☆

SONG _____ **ALBUM** _____

LYRICS YOU LOVE

_____
_____
_____
_____

♡♡♡♡♡
◊◊◊◊◊
♨♨♨♨♨
☆☆☆☆☆

SONG _____ **ALBUM** _____

LYRICS YOU LOVE

_____
_____
_____
_____

♡♡♡♡♡
◊◊◊◊◊
♨♨♨♨♨
☆☆☆☆☆

SONG _____ **ALBUM** _____

LYRICS YOU LOVE

_____
_____
_____
_____

♡♡♡♡♡
◊◊◊◊◊
♨♨♨♨♨
☆☆☆☆☆

SONG _____ **ALBUM** _____

LYRICS YOU LOVE

_____
_____
_____
_____

♡♡♡♡♡
◊◊◊◊◊
♨♨♨♨♨
☆☆☆☆☆

SONG
_____

ALBUM
_____

LYRICS YOU LOVE

_____
_____
_____
_____

♡♡♡♡♡
◊◊◊◊◊
♨♨♨♨♨
☆☆☆☆☆

SONG
_____

ALBUM
_____

LYRICS YOU LOVE

_____
_____
_____
_____

♡♡♡♡♡
◊◊◊◊◊
♨♨♨♨♨
☆☆☆☆☆

SONG
_____

ALBUM
_____

LYRICS YOU LOVE

_____
_____
_____
_____

♡♡♡♡♡
◊◊◊◊◊
♨♨♨♨♨
☆☆☆☆☆

SONG
_____

ALBUM
_____

LYRICS YOU LOVE

_____
_____
_____
_____

♡♡♡♡♡
◊◊◊◊◊
♨♨♨♨♨
☆☆☆☆☆

SONG
_____

ALBUM
_____

LYRICS YOU LOVE

_____
_____
_____
_____

♡♡♡♡♡
◊◊◊◊◊
♨♨♨♨♨
☆☆☆☆☆

SONG
_____

ALBUM
_____

LYRICS YOU LOVE

_____
_____
_____
_____

LYRICS TO LIVE BY

♥ Feeling all the butterflies

💧 Sad-girl mode and hugs during heartbreak

🔥 Power and confidence

★ Straight bangers

♡♡♡♡♡
◊◊◊◊◊
🔥🔥🔥🔥🔥
☆☆☆☆☆

SONG _____

ALBUM _____

LYRICS YOU LOVE

_____
_____
_____
_____

♡♡♡♡♡
◊◊◊◊◊
🔥🔥🔥🔥🔥
☆☆☆☆☆

SONG _____

ALBUM _____

LYRICS YOU LOVE

_____
_____
_____
_____

♡♡♡♡♡
◊◊◊◊◊
🔥🔥🔥🔥🔥
☆☆☆☆☆

SONG _____

ALBUM _____

LYRICS YOU LOVE

_____
_____
_____
_____

♡♡♡♡♡
◊◊◊◊◊
🔥🔥🔥🔥🔥
☆☆☆☆☆

SONG _____

ALBUM _____

LYRICS YOU LOVE

_____
_____
_____
_____

♡ ♡ ♡ ♡ ♡
◌ ◌ ◌ ◌ ◌   **SONG**   **ALBUM**
◌ ◌ ◌ ◌ ◌   _____   _____
☆ ☆ ☆ ☆ ☆   **LYRICS YOU LOVE**

_____

_____

_____

_____

♡ ♡ ♡ ♡ ♡
◌ ◌ ◌ ◌ ◌   **SONG**   **ALBUM**
◌ ◌ ◌ ◌ ◌   _____   _____
☆ ☆ ☆ ☆ ☆   **LYRICS YOU LOVE**

_____

_____

_____

_____

♡ ♡ ♡ ♡ ♡
◌ ◌ ◌ ◌ ◌   **SONG**   **ALBUM**
◌ ◌ ◌ ◌ ◌   _____   _____
☆ ☆ ☆ ☆ ☆   **LYRICS YOU LOVE**

_____

_____

_____

_____

♡ ♡ ♡ ♡ ♡
◌ ◌ ◌ ◌ ◌   **SONG**   **ALBUM**
◌ ◌ ◌ ◌ ◌   _____   _____
☆ ☆ ☆ ☆ ☆   **LYRICS YOU LOVE**

_____

_____

_____

_____

♡ ♡ ♡ ♡ ♡
◌ ◌ ◌ ◌ ◌   **SONG**   **ALBUM**
◌ ◌ ◌ ◌ ◌   _____   _____
☆ ☆ ☆ ☆ ☆   **LYRICS YOU LOVE**

_____

_____

_____

_____

♡ ♡ ♡ ♡ ♡
◌ ◌ ◌ ◌ ◌   **SONG**   **ALBUM**
◌ ◌ ◌ ◌ ◌   _____   _____
☆ ☆ ☆ ☆ ☆   **LYRICS YOU LOVE**

_____

_____

_____

_____

YOUR SQUAD

Celebrate your squad! In the lines below, make a list of the
T-Swift songs and lyrics that remind you of your besties.

SONG _____ ALBUM _____ BESTIE _____

LYRICS _____

STORY BEHIND IT _____

SONG _____ ALBUM _____ BESTIE _____

LYRICS _____

STORY BEHIND IT _____

SONG _____ ALBUM _____ BESTIE _____

LYRICS _____

STORY BEHIND IT _____

SONG _____ ALBUM _____ BESTIE _____

LYRICS _____

STORY BEHIND IT _____

SONG _____ ALBUM _____ BESTIE _____

LYRICS _____

STORY BEHIND IT _____

YOUR LOVES

Celebrate your past romances. Whether they made you think "Today Was a Fairytale," they were the object of your "Wildest Dreams," or they were just another "Picture to Burn," mark them down along with the Taylor Swift song you most associate with the ones you think of most.

SONG _____ ALBUM _____ LOVE _____

LYRICS _____

STORY BEHIND IT _____

SONG _____ ALBUM _____ LOVE _____

LYRICS _____

STORY BEHIND IT _____

SONG _____ ALBUM _____ LOVE _____

LYRICS _____

STORY BEHIND IT _____

SONG _____ ALBUM _____ LOVE _____

LYRICS _____

STORY BEHIND IT _____

SONG _____ ALBUM _____ LOVE _____

LYRICS _____

STORY BEHIND IT _____

YOUR ERAS TOP TEN

Let's be real: The No. 1 song in your heart may not be the same as what appeared on the Billboard charts. Below, list your top ten Taylor tracks of her ten eras. Grade the eras on a scale of one to five hearts, tears, flames, and stars for the songs that had the biggest effect on you or that you just love belting out.

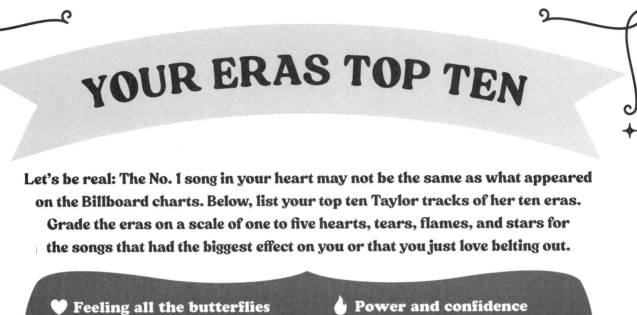

♥ **Feeling all the butterflies**

◊ **Sad-girl mode and hugs during heartbreak**

🔥 **Power and confidence**

★ **Straight bangers**

♡♡♡♡♡
◊◊◊◊◊
🔥🔥🔥🔥🔥
☆☆☆☆☆

SONG

_____

ALBUM

_____

STORY BEHIND IT

_____
_____
_____
_____

♡♡♡♡♡
◊◊◊◊◊
🔥🔥🔥🔥🔥
☆☆☆☆☆

SONG

_____

ALBUM

_____

STORY BEHIND IT

_____
_____
_____
_____

♡♡♡♡♡
◊◊◊◊◊
🔥🔥🔥🔥🔥
☆☆☆☆☆

SONG

_____

ALBUM

_____

STORY BEHIND IT

_____
_____
_____
_____

♡♡♡♡♡
◊◊◊◊◊
🔥🔥🔥🔥🔥
☆☆☆☆☆

SONG

_____

ALBUM

_____

STORY BEHIND IT

_____
_____
_____
_____

♡♡♡♡♡ **SONG**   **ALBUM**
◊◊◊◊◊
♨♨♨♨♨ _____ _____
☆☆☆☆☆ **STORY BEHIND IT**

_____

_____

_____

♡♡♡♡♡ **SONG**   **ALBUM**
◊◊◊◊◊
♨♨♨♨♨ _____ _____
☆☆☆☆☆ **STORY BEHIND IT**

_____

_____

_____

♡♡♡♡♡ **SONG**   **ALBUM**
◊◊◊◊◊
♨♨♨♨♨ _____ _____
☆☆☆☆☆ **STORY BEHIND IT**

_____

_____

_____

♡♡♡♡♡ **SONG**   **ALBUM**
◊◊◊◊◊
♨♨♨♨♨ _____ _____
☆☆☆☆☆ **STORY BEHIND IT**

_____

_____

_____

♡♡♡♡♡ **SONG**   **ALBUM**
◊◊◊◊◊
♨♨♨♨♨ _____ _____
☆☆☆☆☆ **STORY BEHIND IT**

_____

_____

_____

♡♡♡♡♡ **SONG**   **ALBUM**
◊◊◊◊◊
♨♨♨♨♨ _____ _____
☆☆☆☆☆ **STORY BEHIND IT**

_____

_____

_____

THE ERAS AND MORE

Dive deeper into Taylor's world through a closer look at her impact and growth across her eras and time.

THE *TAYLOR SWIFT* ERA

Sixteen sounds like a young age to release your debut album, but for Taylor Swift, there was no time to waste. Taylor broke onto the country music scene after years of discipline, focus, and vision. She knew she wanted to be a singer-songwriter, and she and her family took steps to make it happen. Taylor and her mom shopped demo tapes around Nashville when she was just eleven years old, getting rejections for being too young and not fitting the mold. So she put her head down, focused heavily on improving her piano and guitar skills (practicing so hard her fingers bled), and worked to learn the fundamentals of songwriting through her artist development deal with RCA Records. It wasn't until she was noticed during her performance of "The Star-Spangled Banner" at the US Open in 2003 that she got traction. After one false start with another record label, Taylor signed with Scott Borchetta's new label, Big Machine Records, in 2005.

What came next was the dawn of one of the biggest careers in music history. Taylor released her self-titled album *Taylor Swift* in 2006, writing three songs entirely on her own and having a hand in all the rest. Taylor's unique approach to country—her firm belief that a teenage girl with teenage problems has an audience in an industry dominated by adults—was something no one was ready for. Even with the influence of fan favorites like Shania Twain, Faith Hill, and The Chicks, Taylor's fresh take on country (including promoting her music on her Myspace page, much to the confusion of the adults in the room) made her revolutionary in the industry. Songs like "Picture to Burn," "Teardrops on My Guitar," and "Our Song" carved out an entirely new space in the country audience, one that could cross over to the mainstream and fill the ears of teens everywhere, who could relate. Taylor opened for big acts like Tim McGraw, Faith Hill, George Strait, and Brad Paisley. Her efforts would not go unnoticed. *Taylor Swift* was nominated for Album of the Year at the 2008 Academy of Country Music Awards, and she took home the award for Best New Female Vocalist.

THE *FEARLESS* ERA

This is the era of rhinestones, ballgowns, and heart hands. As Taylor gained better footing in her cowboy boots with her new album, *Fearless*, released on November 11, 2008, she was also connecting with a new generation of music through the combination of her crooning vocals and fairytale lyrics, making her a country pop darling. This was Taylor's first experience as a producer on an album, and she is credited as the sole songwriter on seven of the thirteen tracks. (Lucky #13.) Songs like "You Belong With Me" turned the universally vulnerable ideas of out-of-reach love and popularity into a fun, encouraging anthem, while "Love Story" flipped the Romeo and Juliet tragic romance on its head with a happy ending. Taylor embodied girlhood and the everyday struggles of growing up while her musical peers' songs tended to reside in a more lavish Hollywood universe. Although Taylor had written about real people on her debut album, *Fearless* featured the first songs about famous love interests. "Forever & Always," along with the vault track "Mr. Perfectly Fine," gave fans an eye into her relationship with Jonas Brothers star Joe Jonas.

Fearless is the most-awarded country album of all time, and at twenty, Taylor was the youngest person at the time to receive the Grammys crown for Album of the Year. Infamously, doe-eyed Taylor was on stage receiving a Best Female Video Moonman at the MTV Video Music Awards for "You Belong With Me," only to be interrupted on stage by Kanye West, who grabbed the microphone and told the crowd that Beyoncé deserved the award more for "Single Ladies." This moment would be just the first in a long line of incidents involving the rapper throughout her career, playing into the highs and lows of her reputation as an artist. If music fans weren't paying attention before, Taylor had their attention now.

THE *SPEAK NOW* ERA

Firmly in the country pop space, Taylor's accolades and accomplishments came rolling in as soon as *Speak Now* hit stores in 2010. This was the first album she wrote and produced entirely by herself, and the confessional, sometimes melancholic nature of the album brought fans into a new emotional space with Swift as their guide. The peppy optimism of her earlier albums was offset by themes of heartbreak and regret that showed her maturing themes and growth as an artist. Taylor's lyrics gave fans a look into her relationships, which provided fodder for the tabloid gossip machine as well as fans' voracious consumption of her love life. Clues and insinuations in songs like "Dear John" pointed to heartbreak and feelings of foolishness in her relationship with solo artist John Mayer, while "Back to

December" tuned into feelings of regret and seeking forgiveness, presumably from former boyfriend Taylor Lautner. The song "Innocent" forgave Kanye West for his VMAs indiscretion, an olive branch that Taylor would later look back on as a lesson in not trying so hard to get people to like you for the wrong reasons.

While Taylor was in her *Speak Now* era, she was also expanding her wings beyond her own music. She had her first acting role in the film *Valentine's Day*, she co-wrote music for other artists, and she appeared on the mainstream television circuit with appearances on *CSI* and *Saturday Night Live*, where she became the first host to pen her own opening monologue. As she gained more popularity, not just as a country artist but as a proper star, *Speak Now* collected award after award and broke sales records, despite the new and uncertain era of tanking CD sales with the dawn of "free" (read: illegal) downloads online.

THE *RED* ERA

Country music was not yet in Taylor's rearview, but it became clear with 2012's *Red* that a new genre of music was on her horizon. Critics couldn't make sense of the mix of country sounds and blips of pop music, and the initial critical reception for the album was lukewarm if not, well, critical. This autumnal album introduced fans to Taylor's favorite season, along with what would become her statement red lipstick and more mature presence. The song "We Are Never Ever Getting Back Together" defied critics and landed Taylor at the top spot of the Billboard Hot 100 for the first time. Not only was it a pop song, but it was an in-your-face breakup anthem that fans would determine was about Jake Gyllenhaal.

While other songs like "All Too Well" and "I Knew You Were Trouble" stirred suspicions about her love life, Taylor received not-so-subtle pushback for her vulnerable, diaristic storytelling in real life. In a now-viral clip of one interview on *Ellen*, host Ellen DeGeneres grilled Taylor on her dating life, forcing her to ring a bell any time someone she dated popped up on the screen behind her. What was seen as a funny bit in the early 2010s is now a giant red flag signaling a time when women were relentlessly publicly humiliated for their private lives and held to unfair double standards. This moment, among many others, would fuel Taylor's later professional and personal endeavors to upend this norm. All the while, and perhaps relatedly, Taylor's budding friendships with her "Squad," including Karlie Kloss, the sisters of HAIM, Cara Delavigne, and Lena Dunham, came into focus.

THE *1989* ERA

In her pop era, Taylor hit a brand-new level of fame with a mainstream album that saw new, maturing sides of the artist. Full of speculation-friendly songs that would let fans wonder about her various romances, including the sizzling Harry Styles, the album was also self-aware, funny, and parodied what the critics said about her. "Blank Space" directly snubbed the idea that she should be embarrassed of her dating history while "Shake It Off" looked her critics in the face and deemed them unworthy. "Bad Blood" was both the proud ballad that showed off her strong friendships with her squad, as well as a clunky power move during her purported feud with Katy Perry that some fans perceived as bullying.

While this album saw the beginnings of Taylor's ascendance to superstardom through showstopping performances and popcorn-worthy hints at her love life, it was also a slow, years-long tectonic shift in her advocacy, agency, credibility, and cultural influence. During the subsequent years, she faced a multitude of personal and public hurdles. When Spotify's policies continued to strangle artists' abilities to collect better-than-flimsy royalties, Taylor pulled her music off the platform, taking a stand on behalf of artists to uphold their worth. When Apple Music toyed with artist royalties during a streaming promotion in 2015, Taylor wrote an open letter speaking up for artists and singlehandedly changed the policy. Publicly, these moves were both praised and criticized—she was perceived as too much, too controlling, and too greedy for a pop artist when moves by comparable male artists would have been applauded. At the same time, the political climate in the United States was boiling over, and a particularly vile section of the Internet claimed Taylor as their "Aryan Goddess," who represented racist values. Previously apolitical in public and resistant to making statements on social issues for fear of polarizing her fanbase, Taylor had to come to terms with the influence and power she now had as megastar. In silence, she was complicit, but that era was about to end.

If that weren't enough, Kanye West released the song "Famous" in 2016 and included a line that was both misogynistic and incendiary. Taylor publicly refuted the idea that she'd approved the line, which led Kanye's then wife, Kim Kardashian, to release an edited recording of Taylor during which she seemingly gave her blessing. Turning fans against Taylor with a simple snake emoji, Kimye put the nail in the coffin of Taylor's dying reputation. And with that, the extraordinary success of *1989* faded (temporarily) into the background.

THE *REPUTATION* ERA

After rising to the top, Taylor crashed—hard. In the lead-up to her sixth studio album, and the last one she would record with Big Machine, Taylor sunk into the shadows and dealt with the dark sides of fame and fragile reputations. She refers to this part of her life as the lowest she's ever felt. As she assessed her surroundings and looked back on what had brought her down, Taylor wrote the comeback album that would see her rise from the ashes. *Reputation* had an explosive attitude, and in 2017, it was unlike anything she had released before. "I Did Something Bad" played up her supposedly conniving image, uttering the first but not last swear on any of her albums, and "Look What You Made Me Do" was a powerhouse of a song that clapped back at Kanye West and Kim Kardashian's smear campaign. Not only did Taylor embrace the snake image that had once been used against her, but she also flooded the music video with other hints at her personal struggles. In one scene, she lies in a bathtub filled with diamonds, with a singular dollar bill resting on top. Ever the mastermind, this symbolism likely reflected the $1 Taylor requested in damages during her 2017 sexual assault case. As the tides began to turn in her favor, Taylor relished a new relationship with English actor Joe Alwyn. *Reputation* featured the songs "...Ready For It," "End Game," and "Delicate," among others, which were the first of many lyrical odes to the newfound relationship that would last for more than six years.

Taylor returned to Spotify. Her act of defiance in 2014 helped change the conversation for artists' compensation. Her record contract with Big Machine was about to expire and Taylor was hitting a wall regarding the ownership of the master recordings of her first six albums. The record company wanted her to sign on for more albums in order to acquire ownership, while she felt she'd given them plenty as the major source of the label's revenue. She moved over to Republic Records with Universal Music, where she negotiated a fifty percent royalty and full ownership of her music and publishing rights. This was a big win for Taylor, and it's one that has set an example for other recording artists. But it wasn't over. In 2019, Scott Borchetta sold Big Machine to Scooter Braun, effectively handing total control of Taylor's music over to someone she despised. Shortly after she publicly expressed her grief, Kelly Clarkson tweeted at Taylor advising her to rerecord her albums to regain control of what was rightfully hers. It wasn't unheard of, but no one ever did it because rerecording beloved albums to sound *exactly* as they did when fans fell in love with them was a colossal undertaking. But this advice changed everything.

THE *LOVER* ERA

The soft side of Taylor returned in 2019. Her pastel-colored album, *Lover*, was full of gorgeous, lilting tracks about being in love, feeling at peace, standing up for what she believes in, and tending to different kinds of heartache. During her mother's battle with cancer, Taylor wrote "Soon You'll Get Better" to process her feelings of fear and helplessness. In the song, she paints a bleak portrait of halogen-lit hospital rooms, clusters of orange pill bottles, and heartbreak hanging in the air. While fans connected with the vulnerability of this sensitive song, pop songs like "You Need to Calm Down" and "The Man" also showed her standing her ground and flipping double standards.

Her celebration of her LGBTQ+ fans on the album firmly announced where she stood regarding the social issues on she had previously been quiet. In the 2020 documentary *Miss Americana*, which she directed and starred in, Taylor cleared up questions about her motives and parsed through the years of strict management that curated and controlled her public image as a benign good girl. The film also gave fans an up-close-and-personal look at the very real dangers of her level of fame, including her tearful references to being a victim of stalking. This documentary was a salve on the still healing wound of her reputation, and it set her up for success during the 2020 COVID-19 pandemic.

THE *FOLKLORE* ERA

On July 24, 2020, Taylor released her first of two "quarantine" albums. *Folkore* was a complete sonic departure from all of her previous records, full of softer, mellow songs with electro-acoustic and indie influence. Recorded remotely during a time of lockdowns, escapism, nostalgia, and a dark collective mood, Taylor recorded the vocals in Los Angeles while BFF Jack Antonoff produced the music in New York. Collaborators on the album included beloved indie artist Bon Iver, as well as Taylor's longtime partner, Joe Alwyn, who received songwriting credits as "William Bowery." This album was consumed hungrily by fans stuck at home during the pandemic. The release solidified Taylor as an enduring artist whose well of creativity seemed endless and someone who could ebb and flow with changing genre appetites.

Of the songwriting styles Taylor explored in this album, two of her three "genre pens" made their mark with "quill" songs that felt windswept and of another time like, "The Last Great American Dynasty," and "fountain pen" songs like "My Tears Ricochet." The latter delved into her grief in the aftermath of her professional breakup with Scott Borchetta of Big Machine. The song examines her conflicting feelings of love and betrayal, all while marking the moment in time when she could let go. After two albums with multiple nominations but no major trophies, *Folklore* was the bestselling album of 2020 and won a Grammy for Album of the Year.

THE *EVERMORE* ERA

But wait, there's more. The year 2020 was a blur for everyone stuck in quarantine, but Taylor's albums were stabilizing forces. December 11's *Evermore* was a continuation of the gentle sounds of *Folklore* and even carried some of its narrative arcs along with it. This second quarantine album featured Bon Iver and The National contributing to the dreamy, escapist quality of its sounds and themes, while HAIM's support in "No Body, No Crime," had throwback energy to twangy, country-music-style vengeance.

Taylor spent the first year of the pandemic churning out new music, but she didn't forget her past. In February of 2021, she began rerecording her first albums to regain control of her ownership and profits. She dropped *Fearless (Taylor's Version)* in April 2021 and then *Red (Taylor's Version)* in November. This was the beginning of a completely unprecedented revival of her earlier recordings, many of which performed better the second time around. Most prominently was "All Too Well," which was not a chart-topper upon its first release, but had endeared itself to fans over the years. The rerelease of this song on November 12, 2021, stopped time with the accompanying, *All Too Well: The Short Film*, starring Sadie Sink of *Stranger Things* fame. The 10-minute version invigorated nostalgia, stirred up rumors, and was one of many surprises to come from the Taylor Swift box of goodies.

THE *MIDNIGHTS* ERA

Things. Just. Got. Interesting. On October 21, 2022, Taylor's hotly anticipated new album delivered. Each time fans got comfortable with the track list, Taylor announced new and extended versions of the album, ending up with *Midnights (3am Edition)*, *Midnights (Til Dawn Edition)*, and more. It didn't stop there. Backed by her creative freedom, financial autonomy, and steadfast fanbase, there was no need to stick to industry norms when a song didn't go over well. When fans complained that they couldn't hear Lana del Rey in "Snow on the Beach," Taylor went back to the song and rereleased the "More Lana" version. This willingness to shift, rewrite, and surprise has become Taylor's calling card with every "Taylor's Version." The track list featured intimate songs about her relationship with Joe Alwyn but also hinted at its cracks. The album was a critical success, with raw, self-reflective, and self-affirming songs that built up to the unstoppable force of her Eras Tour.

In some ways, the dawn of the Eras Tour was the ending of one Taylor and the beginning of another. Just ahead of her Florida show, her breakup with longtime partner, Joe Alwyn, became public. But Taylor just started breaking every record *never* imagined. Ticket sales broke Ticketmaster, her concerts caused "amnesia" among fans, and at one point, she made truly astounding history by filling the entire Top 10 list of the Billboard Hot 100 with her songs from multiple albums, with "Anti-Hero" claiming the top spot. The Eras Tour earned $1 billion in revenue in its first leg, making it the highest-grossing tour of all time and causing spikes in the local economy of every city it touched. She released *Speak Now (Taylor's Version)* and *1989 (Taylor's Version)* to outlandish success. When the film industry came screeching to a halt due to writer and actor strikes, Taylor funded her own film and followed strike demands when she released *Taylor Swift: The Eras Tour*, so fans who couldn't attend her show could see it in theaters. She became *Time* magazine's "Person of the Year" for 2023. Oh, and she found new love with Kansas City football player Travis Kelce. Everything's coming up Taylor, and her limitless efforts were rewarded with accolade upon accolade, including Best Pop Vocal Album and Album of the Year at the 2024 Grammy Awards.

AND MORE. . .

On February 4, 2024, Taylor dropped a surprise announcement for her eleventh album, *The Tortured Poets Department*. While her fans read all the initial tea leaves to mean she'd be dropping *Reputation (Taylor's Version)*, they were wrong. Instead, she promised to spill the English tea with an album dripping in hints bidding farewell to "London." As she stood on stage at the Grammys, Taylor deftly removed her opera gloves and announced the album fans didn't know they'd been awaiting for two years.

When Taylor was interviewed by *Time* magazine for Person of the Year, she commented, "I've been raised up and down the flagpole of public opinion so many times in the last twenty years. I've been given a tiara, then had it taken away." What makes Taylor an enduring legacy creator in the industry is her ability to shift, recover, and reinvent herself while always keeping her eyes on her fans. With the shedding of snake skins, friends, boyfriends, and bad deals, Taylor may just have stepped into an entirely new kind of era. The unapologetic one. The one where the gloves come off and the jewels come on.

Solutions

Pages 14–15
BEGINNINGS

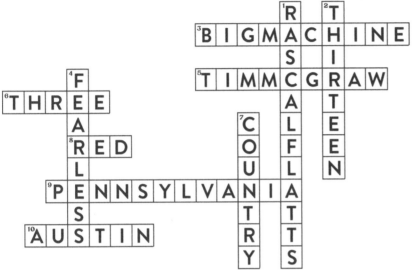

Across:
3. BIG MACHINE
5. TIM MCGRAW
6. THREE
8. RED
9. PENNSYLVANIA
10. AUSTIN

Down:
1. RASCALFLATTS
2. THIRTEEN
4. FEARLESS
7. COUNTRY

Pages 18–19
TAYLOR'S SQUAD WORD SEARCH

Pages 20–21

SONGS FOR SWIFTIES

- "Picture to Burn"
- "You Belong With Me"
- "Enchanted"
- "All Too Well"
- "Wildest Dreams"
- "Look What You Made Me Do"
- "The Man"
- "My Tears Ricochet"
- "Champagne Problems"
- "Snow on the Beach"

Pages 22–23

SHE'S NUMBER ONE

- "Shake It Off"
- "Blank Space"
- "Bad Blood" (featuring Kendrick Lamar)
- "Look What You Made Me Do"
- "Cardigan"
- "Willow"
- "Anti-Hero"
- "Cruel Summer
- "Is It Over Now? (Taylor's Version)"
- "We Are Never Ever Getting Back Together"

Page 26

FOR THE LOVE OF HER GUITAR

Deering Boston 6-String Banjo—"Mean"

Sparkly Swarovski Crystal Taylor GS6 Grand Symphony Acoustic Guitar—"Fearless"

Taylor Living Jewels Koi Acoustic Guitar—"Last Kiss"

Embellished Red Sparkly Gibson Les Paul Special SL—"Red"

1959 Silvertone 605 Acoustic Guitar—"the 1"

Pages 28–29

DAZZLING DISCOGRAPHY WORD SEARCH

```
T N S S E L R A E F E Y
A W O N K A E P S N W L
Y R X I J Y P D I W T Q
L R N Q T D Y N G S Z E
O E L E D A Y L T Y R W
R K V P E T T H G O X Q
S D M E H T G U L N B G
W Z Z G R I E K P L R T
I Q I Y N M L N O E Q Q
F E R D T O O V I P R J
T Y I E F W E R K N Y V
V M L G D R P B E D N Q
```

Pages 34–35

HOLLYWOOD STAR

Pages 36–37

SONGS FOR SWIFTIES

1. "Our Song"
2. "Fifteen"
3. "Dear John"
4. "The Last Time"
5. "Bad Blood"
6. "New Year's Day"
7. "Soon You'll Get Better"
8. "Betty"
9. "Willow"
10. "Lavender Haze"

Pages 38–39

RAISING HER VOICE WORD SEARCH

Pages 46–47

IT'S NOT ALL HEARTS AND ROMANCE

1. "The Best Day"
2. "Ronan"
3. "The Man"
4. "My Tears Ricochet"
5. "Marjorie"
6. "Epiphany"
7. "Seven"
8. "Innocent"
9. "The Last Great American Dynasty"
10. "Mad Woman"

Page 48

PIANO MAGIC

Mossy grand piano—Folklore set

Wooden upright with floral accents—Surprise acoustic set

Black-and-white grand piano with woodgrain pattern—Reputation set

Silver sparkly grand piano—Formula 1 United States Grand Prix performance in 2016

Gold-and-pink grand piano with filigree adornments—American Music Awards performance in 2019

Page 50

CHECK HER REPUTATION

- Kanye West
- Beyoncé
- "Innocent"
- Kim Kardashian
- A snake

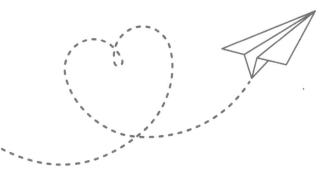

Pages 54–55

RANDOM ACTS OF TAYNESS CROSSWORD

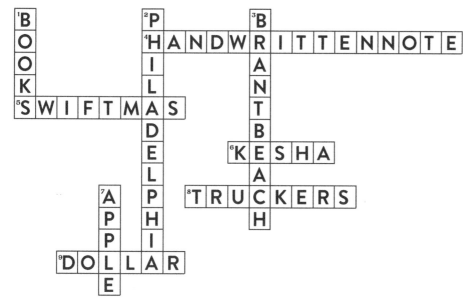

¹BOOKS

²PHILADELPHIA

³BRANTBEACH

⁴HANDWRITTENNOTE

⁵SWIFTMAS

⁶KESHA

⁷APPLE

⁸TRUCKERS

⁹DOLLAR

Pages 58–59

TAYLOR'S LOVES WORD SEARCH

```
J T R A V I S K E L C E J V T
A N A H A R R Y S T Y L E S D
K O L Y J O E J O N A S D T C
E T Z W L X R K J Z Y Y Z A Z
G S P J D O K E R D N K L V N
Y E V V N L R Q Y Y B V J G J
L L B D J M G L W A I D G P P
L I D R N G X Y L A N M T N Z D
E I D L R Y G A X H U L N Z Y R
N I T D X E D A K L T Y H Y M
H H Y D Q O R V R W M N J O P
A M K J N R Y V X R D W E X J
A O B L I D B J K N P D M R B
L T T S G Y R X R K N D M Q W
```

95